# On Coming!

## Faith Talk

## W. Dean Witten

**Dedicated to the Glory of God**


**In gratitude**


**For Our Church Family**

## ATTRIBUTIONS .

Scripture verses quoted from the New Revised Standard Version Bible. "New Revised Standard Version Bible, copyright 1989, Division of Christian Education of the National Council of the Churches of Christ in the United States of America. Used by permission. All rights reserved."

Cover Image is copyrighted and used by permission of Shutterstock, photo ID: 79215718.

Image, pages 18 & 66 source unknown.

Images ID: 156429383 (Page 43),243657676 (Page 76) Used by permission of Shutterstock.

Complimentary editing services provided by Wendell Witten and Lisa Witten Williams.

ISBN-13: 978-1721670789
ISBN-10: 1721670785

Copyright July 2018

# Copyright

## ABOUT THE AUTHOR

W. Dean Witten is a 1960 graduate of Florida Southern College with a Bachelor of Arts degree and a 1963 graduate of the Methodist Theological School in Ohio with a Master of Divinity degree. Florida Southern also honored him with a Doctor of Divinity degree.

Rev. Witten was ordained an elder and granted full membership in the Florida Annual Conference of The United Methodist Church In 1964. He has since served as pastor of seven United Methodist churches. In addition, he served as superintendent of the Sarasota and Orlando districts of the Florida Conference UMC, 1992 to 2002. After 41 years of service he retired in June 2002.

**Books Written by W. Dean Witten**

Does God Really Care About Me?
Connecting the Dots

God's Story: Advent & Christmas

God's Story: Good Friday & Easter

Living Through the Storms: Job's Story

Questions for God: Seeking Clarity

Jesus' Questions for Present Day Christians

Praying Like Jesus through the Storms of Life

Living in an Unsafe World: Reflections on
Psalm 23

The Beatitudes of Jesus

The King is Coming: Advent & Christmas

The King is Coming: Epiphany

The King is Coming: Lent

The King is Coming: Easter

The King is Coming: Pentecost

These books are available at
Amazon.com, CreateSpace.com, and
other retail outlets.

# Table of Contents

## Preface

Hurricanes are not new to our family. We have weathered many of these destructive storms through the years. Thank God, we have not lost any family members to a raging storm.

As a pastor, I lived through hurricanes and tornadoes when I shepherded congregations in Lakeland, Belleview, Juno Beach, Longwood, and Palm Beach Gardens. Moreover, as a district superintended, I shepherded the Orlando District of the UMC during the tornadoes of 2001.

Like our nation and citizens of Florida, I watched with deep concern as Hurricane Harvey ravaged Houston and nearby Texas cities at the end of August 2017. Inasmuch as my relatives live in these cities, I watched coverage intensely and prayed hard.

The next week, Hurricane Irma was born. She barreled through the Caribbean to Florida. For several days, we were glued to television coverage, hoping Irma would pass us by. She did not, and on Sunday, September 10, 2017, Irma made landfall in South Florida and set out on destructive path up the West Coast.

This book was conceived as Hurricane Irma battered Florida. I'm hopeful these devotions will be helpful for Christians and others passing through violent and destructive storms in the future. Moreover, I pray for the Lord to bless and keep you safe.

Practice the Spiritual Discipline of Journaling

A way to concentrate on being in Christ's presence during a hurricane.

1. Read the devotion/reflection for the day. Record your thoughts and/or write your personal reflections.

2. Be still and prayerfully listen for Christ's message to you. Record what you hear from the Lord.

3. Pray the prayer that is written and/or record and pray your own prayer.

4. Conclude with praise and worship. Use the suggested hymn from YouTube or choose another.

Mark 4:35-41

"On that day, when evening had come, he said to them, 'Let us go across to the other side.' And leaving the crowd behind, they took him with them in the boat, just as he was. Other boats were with him. A great windstorm arose, and the waves beat into the boat, so that the boat was already being swamped. But he was in the stern, asleep on the cushion; and they woke him up and said to him, 'Teacher, do you not care that we are perishing?' He woke up and rebuked the wind, and said to the sea, 'Peace! Be still!' Then the wind ceased, and there was a dead calm. He said to them, 'Why are you afraid? Have you still no faith?' And they were filled with great awe and said to one another, 'Who then is this, that even the wind and the sea obey him?'"

# Before the Storm

## Faith Talk

"Again, truly I tell you, if two of you agree on earth about anything you ask, it will be done for you by my Father in heaven. For where two or three are gathered in my name, I am there among them." Matthew 18:19-20

## Part 1
### "His Promise"

Christ promised in the gospel, "Lo, I am with you always, to the close of the age." Really? Good news to be sure!

That reminds me of a Chinese man whose name was "Lo." He listened intently, as a minister expounded the Word of God during worship service. He became extremely excited when the pastor read these words, "Lo, I am with you always, to the close of the age." Lo's heart danced with joy. "Just think," he exclaimed, "the Lord knows me by name and makes me a promise like that!"[1]

---

1 Guide Posts 1986

19

The good news is that the Lord has made this promise to each of us. Therefore, wherever we go, one thing is sure, namely, that he is with us.

- Skies will grow dark but Jesus says, "Lo, I am with you always."
- Lightening will flash and thunder will rumble but Jesus says, "Lo, I am with you always."
- Winds will be devastating but Jesus says, "Lo, I am with you always."
- Trees will fall and crush houses but Jesus says, "Lo, I am with you always."
- Roofs will be ripped from homes but Jesus says, "Lo, I am with you always."
- Some may be injured and even die but Jesus says, "Lo, I am with you always."

Amen.

## Christ Among Us!

### "Where does Christ meet us today?"

Jesus said, "Where two or three are gathered in my name, I am there among them." Matthew 18:20

When the church family gathers for worship, Christ is "among them." He does not say, "I will be there if ten thousand show up." Only two or three are needed.

Only two or three? Yes, of course, only two or three.

• When a small prayer group meets in his name, Christ is "there among them."

• When members of the church family visit each other in the hospital, Christ is "there (in the hospital room) among them."

• When a family meets around the dinner table in his name, Christ is "there among them."

• When you and your spouse are in the storm, Christ is there "among you."

• Etcetera! Etcetera! Etcetera!

Let the reader pause and visualize all the places where "two or three are gathered together in my (his) name."

Where two or three are gathered together in his name, Christ is "there among them." Period! No exceptions!

Let us acknowledge and claim his presence among us during the storm and give him the glory. Amen.

Pray

Dear Jesus, now that you are among us, heal our sick and give hope to all who despair. Moreover, where faith is weak, make it strong; where vision is dim, renew it; where hope is fragile, reinforce mind and spirit with your unconditional love. Bless our church family with a special dispensation of your grace and mercy. Amen

Sing and/or Listen
"Jesus, The Very Thought of Thee"
https://www.youtube.com/watch?v=9Vr8jsOx0
Co

"Jesus, the very thought of thee
with sweetness fills the breast;
but sweeter far thy face to see,
and in thy presence rest.

"O hope of every contrite heart,
O joy of all the meek,
to those who fall, how kind thou art!
How good to those who seek!

"But what to those who find? Ah, this
nor tongue nor pen can show;
the love of Jesus, what it is,
none but his loved ones know.

"Jesus, our only joy be thou,
as thou our prize wilt be;
Jesus, be thou our glory now,
and through eternity."
Bernard of Clairvaux - UM Hymnal, Number 175

Practice the Spiritual Discipline of Journaling

A way to concentrate on being in Christ's presence during a hurricane.

1. Read the devotion/reflection for the day. Record your thoughts and/or write your personal reflections.

2. Be still and prayerfully listen for Christ's message to you. Record what you hear from the Lord.

3. Pray the prayer that is written and/or record and pray your own prayer.

4. Conclude with praise and worship. Use the suggested hymn from YouTube or choose another.

Part 2

Christ among us!

"For where two or three are gathered in my name, I am there among them." Matthew 18: 20

### "Only Two or Three Needed"

A retired navy man shared the story of his visit to the Civil Air Patrol office in a small Florida town. They had a radio which received messages in Morse Code simultaneously from several sources. At first it sounded like firecrackers on the fourth of July. Gradually, however, he began to pick out different signals. One was high, another low; one staccato, another slower. There was one gentle signal so slow that even his rusty Morse Code skills could pick it up. When he tuned out the others and concentrated on that slower signal, he got the message.

Christians are bombarded by signals that compete for our attention. They come from advertiser, politicians, news commentators, and others. The most important of all, however, are the signals from the lips of Jesus Christ through the gospel.

In the gospel verse, he signals us, "For where two or three are gathered in my name, I am there among them."

When the church family gathers on Sunday morning, Christ is among us. He does not say, "I will be there if you invite me." Nor does he say, "I will be there if ten thousand show up." Only two or three are needed.

## Pray

Dear Jesus, now that you are among us, save us. We are tempted to sing solo, to disrupt the flow of the song, to refuse to sing altogether. We head out to the beach to chant with lonely voices to the sands, and, although we are met by their silence, we would sometime choose to sit alone among the shifting dunes rather than stand with the chorus upon the rock.

Lord, save us. When our words are not your words and our ways are not your ways, we are grateful that your voice speaks your Word to us individually and to the church family.

Help us, Lord, to focus on and hear your Word as the storms come. Amen.

Listen and/or Sing
"Wonderful Words of Life"
https://www.youtube.com/watch?v=0j1f5Tdj-tk

"1. Sing them over again to me,
wonderful words of life;
let me more of their beauty see,
wonderful words of life;
words of life and beauty
teach me faith and duty.
Refrain:
"Beautiful words, wonderful words,
wonderful words of life.
Beautiful words, wonderful words,
wonderful words of life.
"2. Christ, the blessed one, gives to all
wonderful words of life;
sinner, listen to the loving call,
wonderful words of life;
all so freely given,
wooing us to heaven."

Phillip P. Bliss, The United Methodist Hymnal

Part 3

Christ among us.

Christ even meets with and welcomes inmates incarcerated in a county jail.

Matthew 18: 20 "For where two or three are gathered in my name, I am there among them."

"And the Pharisees and the scribes were grumbling and saying, 'This fellow welcomes sinner and eats with them.'" Luke 15:2

### "The Radical Hospitality of Christ"

No one is beyond the love of Christ! He welcomes all who welcome him into their live.

Several years ago, Hazel and Martha met every Friday night to lead a Bible study for a small group of inmates at the local county jail. Hazel often said to me, "Christ met with us." That is of course what Jesus promised. "Where two or three are gathered in my name, I am there among them."

Christ welcomes inmates as well as all others. Don't underestimate the hospitality of Christ. Here is a story to help us get the feel for the full scope of it.

One day, Betty was baking cookies when she received a telephone call. "What are you doing?" asked the friend. "Baking cookies," she replied. "How are you dressed?" the caller inquired. "I'm in an old pair of slacks, blouse and apron," she answered. "Why, what is going on?" Her friend responded, "I'm having a come as you are party and I want you to come. Now, I know what you are wearing and you can't cheat." When she hung up the phone, Betty looked at herself in the mirror. "I can't go looking like this," she declared. Finally, she got up the courage to go and was warmly received.

Jesus Christ is like the telephone caller in that story. His invitation is unconditional. "Come as you are." All are welcome. One need not wait until one has cleaned up one's life, put everything in order, dressed in respectability. The door is open to all who will come and gather in his name.

Christ welcomed Hazel and Martha and the inmates into his presence at a county jail over fifty years ago. He has since welcomed some of them into heaven. His hospitality is radical hospitality.

Jesus said, "Where two or three are gathered in my name, I am there among them." This includes prisoners and other sinners. This even includes you and me when we are gathered together in his name.

## Pray

Dear Jesus! Even though you are among us when we gather for worship, we recognize that all is not well in the world beyond our church. Some are imprisoned, rejected, and discriminated against by society. We acknowledge that when they gather in your name, you are among them. Bless them and send more people like Hazel and Martha to minister to them in your name. Amen.

Sing and/or Listen, "Just as I Am"
https://www.youtube.com/watch?v=_gGBMv42dJY

Part 4

Christ among us.

"For where two or three are gathered in my name, I am there among them."

Matthew 18: 20

In response to Christ's gracious invitation we gather in his name. And he says, "I am there among you."

Why does he promise this? Is it because we are deserving? No! The reality is that we are like little Jeremy who disobeyed his mother. She told him not to go near the creek. He disobeyed. Unfortunately, he accidentally fell into the creek. He panicked and ran home all wet and scared!

Mother saw him coming and met him. He was walking slowly, as if resigned to be wet and miserable in the cold wintry afternoon. He was dripping with creek water and mud from his head to his shoes. Mother led him into the house, undressed and put him into a warm tub of water.

"Why are you crying?" she asked tenderly. "Are you hurt?"

Finally, he looked into her eyes and asked, "Are you glad to see me?"

She replied, "Oh, yes, Jeremy, I'm so glad to see you!"

He just wasn't quite sure so he said, "Even though these were my new clothes and you told me not to go near the creek?"

She said, "That doesn't matter. You are safe and here with me. That's what I care about."

Jesus Christ is like that mother. He cares that you are with him and safe. That's the reality through the storm when only two or three are gathered in his name.

That's why we love him, because he first loved us unconditionally. A storm, however vicious, cannot separate us from him. Parise God!

## Pray

Loving Jesus! Even in our limited understanding of life, we stand in awe of your presence with us. It's like the air we breathe to sustain us, like the sun that warms us, like the raindrops that renew us. Wherever we look, wherever we are, whatever we do, we experience your great mercy.

Help us now, to know your presence more deeply, to sense your mercy more deeply, and to know the peace and healing which come from your unconditional kindness.

Listen and/or Sing, "What Wondrous Love"

https://www.youtube.com/watch?v=DsVnvN3EVxY

Part 5

Christ among us

Why does Christ choose to be among us?

"For where two or three are gathered in my name, I am there among them." Matthew 18: 20

### "He Is Here"

We gather together in his name. Now comes the good news from the lips of Jesus Christ. "Where two or three are gathered in my name, I am there among them."

Why? Why would he choose to be with people like us through a hurricane? Certainly, not because we love him so much but because he loves us. There's no other reason, just his incredible love.

Here's a story about Jana to help us get the feel for it. When she was eleven, her brother was fourteen. His greatest delight, as for many older brothers, was teasing his little sister. The taunts and comments often led her to tears. One day when the teasing became too much, Jana screamed, "I love you Alan," in a voice loud enough to be heard throughout the house. "Sometimes, you try to keep me from it," she cried, "but you can't stop me from loving you. " With tears streaming down her face, she fled to her room, leaving Alan speechless'

Jesus Christ is like Jana. You cannot stop him from loving you. The cross stands as a symbol of the depth and constancy of his love. The fact is that he will not let go of us in his heart. As we sometimes sing in the hymn, "And from my stricken heart with tears two wonders I confess. The wonders of redeeming love and my un-worthiness." UMH, Number 297

Before the hurricane arrives, Christ is among us, not because we love him so much, but because he loves us so much.

Does this mean we have nothing to worry about? Well, a major hurricane is reason to worry about property and even life itself, but we need not worry about the storm blocking or destroying the presence of Christ with us. He will keep his promise. Nothing can change that.

## Pray

O Lord Jesus! Since you love us so much, we have come this day to lift up our minds and thoughts to you, and to answer you with our humble worship. Move us by the strong joyful tone of your truth, so that the hymns and prayers may express adoration and praise, joy and hope, and your name may be exalted above every name.

## Sing and/or Listen

Jesus Loves Me
https://www.youtube.com/watch?v=AQVOId9XFkM

Part 6

Christ among us!

Matthew 18: 20

"For where two or three are gathered in my name, I am there among them."

Luke 5:17-26

"One day, while he was teaching, Pharisees and teachers of the law were sitting nearby (they had come from every village of Galilee and Judea and from Jerusalem); and the power of the Lord was with him to heal. Just then some men came, carrying a paralyzed man on a bed. They were trying to bring him in and lay him before Jesus; but finding no way to bring him in because of the crowd, they went up on the roof and let him down with his bed through the tiles into the middle of the crowd in front of Jesus. When he saw their faith, he said, 'Friend, your sins are forgiven you.' Then the scribes and the Pharisees began to question, 'Who is this who is speaking blas-phemies? Who can forgive sins but God alone?' When Jesus perceived their questionings, he an-swered them, 'Why do you raise such questions in your hearts? Which is easier, to say, your sins are forgiven you, or to say, stand up and walk? But so that you may know that the Son of Man has authority on earth to forgive sins —he said to the one who was paralyzed—I say to you, stand up and take your bed and go to your home.' Immediately he stood up before them, took what he had been lying on, and went to his home, glorifying God. Amazement seized all of them, and they glorified God and were filled with awe, saying, 'We have seen strange things to-day.'"

### "Just Imagine"

Imagine it! "Where two or three are gath-ered together in my name." The Lord is present with the gift of forgiveness in his hands. This means there is another chance for you. As it is written in holy scripture, "If we confess our sin, he is just and will forgive us."

Here is an analogy for clarity. When one makes a typographical error in a Word document, one does not have to retype the document from the beginning to end to make the correction. Instead, one need only highlight the word and retype it; the person reading the sentence has no idea that a mistake was made.

Christ who is in our midst does that for us. Think about it like this. No one is perfect. We have made mistakes and continued to disobey the commandments of God. But, Christ, through his forgiveness, deletes the mistake through his blood the on the cross. The mistake/sin is replaced by him with the word, forgiven.

Pray

Dear Jesus, our Savior and Redeemer! As long as we live on this earth, we will sing your praise. As long as there is breath in our lungs, we will tell of your wonderful work on the cross. Until the day we die, we will glory in your holy name. Even though storms come, we will continue to give thanks because your goodness and steadfast love endures forever. Amen

Listen and/or Sing

"Forgiven"

https://www.youtube.com/watch?v=WJ2Del_Y0CA

Part 7

Christ among us!

"For where two or three are gathered in my name, I am there among them." Matthew 18:20

"Jesus said to her, 'I am the resurrection and the life. Those who believe in me, even though they die, will live.'" John 11:25

"Christ with us"

The Lord is among us. "Where two or three are gathered in my name," Jesus promised. He is here with the gift of hope in his hands as the storm barrels toward us. See it there in his words, "Because I live, you will live also."

I once purchased a time management program which was named "On Time." When I wanted to call on a parishioner in the future, I just set the day and time. When that date arrived, the computer would chime a message and flash the person's name on the screen.

The unexpected happened one day. I set the time incorrectly on the computer program. Later, I reviewed the date of the appointment. It was set for Thursday, September 3, 2065. On that day, I was scheduled to call Gladys Thompson who was in a nursing home.

The problem is that neither Gladys nor I will be on this earth to keep the appointment. She will be dead and so will I. Yet, the Lord Jesus Christ who is among us now will be among us then in heaven. Thus, we sing, "Because he lives, I can face tomorrow."

The good news is Christ among us, "I am there among them." That is true as long as we live on planet earth; that is also true when we transition to the Father's house. Amen

Listen and/or Sing
"Because He Lives"
https://www.youtube.com/watch?v=spa7WkwjwGw
Pray
Thank you, dear Jesus, for being among us. Thank you for the assurance that one day we will

be with you in your Father's house. In the mean-time, I will lean on your presence during this storm and all other times of danger. Amen

During the Storm

Faith Talk

Part 1

Faith talk while waiting for the Hurricane!

Psalm 23:4 "Yea, though I walk through the valley of the shadow of death, I will fear no evil: for thou art with me; thy rod and thy staff they comfort me." KJV

## "Waiting for the Storm"

The storm is coming. We don't know the destruction that is ahead. We do not know whether the days will be good or bad. But one thing we do know: the lord is with us and he holds us in his hands.

When the calm weather returns, and once more I get control of myself, may I, as the disciples after the storm on the Sea of Galilee, stand in awe of the mercy of the Good Shepherd and give him the glory. He is with me.

We don't know what lies ahead of us, but we do know who is with us through it all. The Good Shepherd is! "And remember," he said, "I am with you always, to the end of the age."

Sing and/or listen

"O Happy Day"
https://www.youtube.com/watch?v=55O19Z6K_YE

Pray

O Lord, send your protection to all who are in Storm's path. You know the names of the little children who are in harm's way. You also know the names of their mothers and fathers, brothers and sisters, grandmothers and grandfathers. You also know the names of the poor and the rich, the people with homes and without. Thank you in advance for being with us each and every minute as the storm barrels down on us. Have mercy and deliver us all, O Lord, through your great and wonderful love! Amen!

Practice the Spiritual Discipline of Journaling

A way to concentrate on being in Christ's presence during a hurricane.

1. Read the devotion/reflection for the day. Record your thoughts and/or write your personal reflections.

2. Be still and prayerfully listen for Christ's message to you. Record what you hear from the Lord.

3. Pray the prayer that is written and/or record and pray your own prayer.

4. Conclude with praise and worship. Use the suggested hymn from YouTube or choose another.

Part 2

Faith talk while waiting for the Hurricane!

### "Living in an Unsafe World!"

As Hurricane Irma approached in the summer of 2017, the residents of my community got a foretaste of what was to come. Our community transformer blew up and we were without power for six hours, until 12 A.M. No lights, nor air conditioning, nor cooking, nor TV, nor computer, nor FB.

Imagine that! A foretaste of Irma, without the destruction. All we could do was call out to the Lord and Duke Energy. It was truly a wakeup call!

I remembered and still remember that Psalm 23 is the Lord's gift to people who live in an unsafe world. The good news is that "the Lord is my Shepherd."

As killer hurricane Irma roared toward us, it was good to know that "the Lord is my Shepherd." So, I won't give in to fear as another hurricane roars toward us. Rather, I will choose trust in the Lord and keep on keeping on despite the frightening news of a hurricane's destructive power.

Palm 23 is solid underpinning for people living in an unsafe world.

We may choose to play our hand through the faith that the Lord is with us. In any event, the Lord is my Shepherd.

### Pray

Lord Jesus, we are glad that you are among us. We are fortunate, favored, supported, sustained by your grace. You have come among us, called to us, embraced us, and welcomed us.

Now, we have a hurricane barreling down on us. So, we turn to You, Jesus, our refuge and strength, a very present help in trouble. Have mercy upon us and enfold us with your love, so that during this storm we may experience the tenderness of your presence. Amen.

### Sing and/or Listen
"He's got the whole world in His hand"

https://www.youtube.com/watch?v=IkbHHQtT_Ho

Part 3

Faith talk while waiting for the Hurricane!

"God is our refuge and strength, a very present help in trouble." Psalm 46:1

## "God is our Refuge"

The hurricane is on the way to Florida and/or somewhere else. Nevertheless,"God is still God, regardless of the destructive power the hurricane has already displayed.

• No matter how dark the skies or rough the water, God is still our refuge and strength.
• No matter how long or dark the night, God is still our refuge and strength.
• No matter how severe the destruction, God is still our refuge and strength.
• No matter what the storm threatens, God is still our refuge and strength.

Whatever happens, God is still God. That is the point. Isn't it? God is not old. God is not sick. And God is not tired. The problem is not with God. God is still God regardless of any named storm.

The good news is that "God is our refuge and strength, a very present help in time of trouble."

Pray

O God, our refuge and strength, a very present help in trouble, enfold us with your love, that all who are in the path of this coming storm may experience the tenderness of your presence and the strength of your comforting power. Grant tender hearts to our pastor as he ministers to the church family throughout the storm and beyond. Moreover, give us health in body and soul, that we may endure and bear witness to your goodness and mercy. Amen.

Sing and/or Listen

"How Great Thou Art"

https://www.youtube.com/watch?v=PdE_NKyY_o0

Part 4

Faith talk while waiting for the Hurricane!

"Hope in God; for I shall again praise him, my help and my God." Psalm 42:5

### "Another foretaste of Irma"

Well, it happened again. For the second day in the last week, we lost power in our neighborhood. Irma had not even reached Florida yet, but my neighbors and I have lost our power source. Finally, the power is back, 10:45 AM.

Imagine that! Another foretaste of Irma, without the destruction. All we could do a second time was call out to the Lord and Duke Energy. It was truly a wakeup call!

For most people living in Florida, the question is not whether hurricanes like Irma will invade our state but when.

What to do in the meantime? Prepare and "hope in God." If we do, will Hurricane Irma magically disappear so that we will awaken in the morning and find that Irma has passed us by without inflicting destruction of property and human life? No, it does not mean that at all. Nevertheless, we will choose to prepare and "hope in God."

We will choose hope in God for as long as it takes to be at peace - choose hope when we awaken in the morning; choose hope when we eat lunch at noon; choose hope when we lie down for sleep at night; choose hope when the brutal and destructive winds attack us.

What difference will this make? God will not forsake us! The Lord is our Shepherd. For this reason, when Irma has passed and the calm weather returns, when we regain control of our lives and communities, we will praise God and give God the glory.

"Hope in God; for I shall again praise him, my help and my God." Amen

### Prayer

Lord Jesus, as long as we live on this earth, we will sing your praise.  As long as there is breath in our lungs, we will tell of your wonderful works.  Until the day we die, we will glory in your holy name. Even though the storms come and threaten our existence, we will continue to give thanks because your goodness and steadfast love endures forever.

Sing and/or Listen

"To God Be the Glory"

https://www.youtube.com/watch?v=-15v9iworAU

"To God be the glory, great things he hath
done!
So loved he the world that he gave us his Son,
who yielded his life an atonement for sin,
and opened the life-gate that all may go in.
Praise the Lord, praise the Lord,
let the earth hear his voice!
Praise the Lord, praise the Lord,
let the people rejoice!
O come to the Father through Jesus the Son,
and give him the glory, great things he hath
done!"

-Fanny J. Crosby,
The United Methodist Hymnal Number 98

Part 5

Faith talk while waiting for Hurricane Irma!

"Be still, and know that I am God!" Psalm 46:10

### "Be Still"

"Be still!" Hard to wrap one's mind and emotions around that as the storm rages toward us, threatening destruction and death.

"Be still," says the Lord. In other words, "step back ... let go ... shut up ... cease fire . . . be patient" Drop your arguments. End your war of words. Just "Be still, and know that I am God."

Good news! God is still God, even as the storm roars toward us. The profound implication of this is illustrated in a touching modern analogy. A mother tried to get her five-year-old son to take a nap. She put him in her bed and lay down beside him, hoping he would fall asleep. Ironically, she fell asleep instead. When she awakened, Luke wasn't beside her. She panicked but to her surprise Luke was sitting in a chair at the end of the bed, watching her.

"Luke, what are you doing?" she exclaimed. "Oh, I'm playing God," he replied. She responded, "You are playing God?" "Yes," he declared. "I'm playing God. I'm watching over you, even while you sleep."

The image of God watching over us is comforting and reassuring in the face of a hurricane. Be still. Slow down and focus on God who is focused on you. That is a powerful and gripping thought. God watches over us, even while we sleep.

### Pray

O Lord, help us to trust that you are watching over us as we pass through the storm. For even our deepest sincerity and enthusiasm, even our greatest attention and good intentions, even the things we know and affirm cannot ensure that we trust you. Have mercy on us and give us faith.

We respectfully request that you send Christ into our midst even now so that the glorious faith of Jesus in your love will become as clear as the shining sun on the brightest day. Let us see what we have not yet seen, know what we have not yet known, and experience that peace of Christ which passes all understanding.

O God, keep us near to your heart. Help us to love you without reservation, to serve you without hesitation, and to trust you with a child's faith. Amen.

Sing and/or Listen

"Be Still and Know"

https://www.youtube.com/watch?v=IC5nxf6Jq7A

## Part 6

Faith talk while waiting for a hurricane!

### "Comfort"

Words of comfort from the Psalms.

- "The Lord is nigh unto them that are of a broken heart." 34:18
- "A lamp unto my feet is your Word, a light to my path." 119:105
- "Only goodness and kindness follow me all the days of my life; and I shall dwell in the house of the Lord for years to come." 23:6
- "I was hard pressed and was falling, but the Lord helped me. My strength and courage is the Lord, and he has been my savior." 118:13-14
- "May the Lord give strength to his people; may the Lord bless his people with peace!" 29:11
- "In peace I will lie down and sleep, for you alone, O LORD, will keep me safe." 4:8

- "May the favor of the Lord our God rest on us; establish the work of our hands for us– yes, establish the work of our hands." 90:17
- "He satisfies the thirsty and fills the hungry with good things." 107:9
- "Blessed be the Lord, who daily loadeth us with benefits, even the God of our salvation. Selah." 68:19
- "The LORD will complete what his purpose is for me. LORD, your gracious love is eternal; do not abandon your personal work in me." 138:8
- "The lines are fallen unto me in pleasant *places*; yea, I have a goodly heritage." 16:6
- "He heals the brokenhearted and binds up their wounds."147:3
- "The LORD sustains them on their sickbed and restores them from their bed of illness." 41:3
- "My flesh and my heart may fail, but God is the strength of my heart and my portion forever." 73:26

- "You are my strength, I sing praise to you; you, God, are my fortress, my God on whom I can rely." 59:17
- "The LORD gives strength to his people; the LORD blesses his people with peace.' 29:11
- "The LORD is my strength and my shield; my heart trusts in him, and he helps me. My heart leaps for joy, and with my song I praise him." 28:7
- "Wait for the LORD; be strong and take heart and wait for the LORD." 27:14
- "Even though I walk through the darkest valley, I will fear no evil, for you are with me; your rod and your staff, they comfort me." 23:4
- "May your unfailing love be my comfort, according to your promise to your servant." 119:76
- "When I am afraid, I will trust in you. In God, whose word I praise, in God I trust; I will not be afraid." 56:3-4

- "From the ends of the earth, I cry to you for help when my heart is overwhelmed. Lead me to the towering rock of safety" 61:2
- "When doubts filled my mind, your comfort gave me renewed hope and cheer." 94:19

Pray

Dear God, we marvel that You have time for us. Yes, in your great love, you listen to us individually and respond to our prayers. We stand amazed. May the mystery of your love delight our hearts and compel us to love You totally and completely.

Send your holy angles to guard us every step of the way, through the bad times as well as the good, in hospitals as well as churches, in the street as well as our homes. Amen

Sing and/or Listen
"He Leadeth Me"
https://www.youtube.com/watch?v=3RGSSj4uIPU

Part 7

Faith talk while waiting for a Hurricane!

### "Why?"

Why does God allow hurricanes? Logic says that a hurricane every now and then will just happen. California has its earthquakes; Arizona has its wildfires; Oklahoma has its tornadoes; West Virginia has its floods; and Florida has its hurricanes.

Ok! But why does God allow damaging hurricanes? We just don't know. We are still waiting for a definitive theological answer to the why question. The reality is that hurricanes just happen.

Here's what we do know, however. Hurricanes come and go, but God is still God! That's the point. Isn't it? Therefore,

- When you don't have the answers and your load is overwhelming, the song says, "take your burden to the Lord and leave it there."

- When you don't know the reason and you are confused, Civillia Martin's song tells you, "Be not dismayed whate'er betide, God will take care of you. . ." And

- When nothing makes sense, Charles Tindley's song assures us that ". . . we'll understand it better by and by." And,

- When life breaks your heart and joy is gone, king David's Psalm promises, "Weeping may linger for the night but joy comes with the morning." Psalm 30:5, And,

- When your soul is restless, the old song tells you to say, "Be still, my soul: the Lord is on your side." And

- When you feel empty inside, Richard Blanchard's song teaches you to pray, "Fill my cup, Lord . . .fill it up and make me whole."

- Jesus said, "Indeed, the very hairs of your head are all numbered. Don't be afraid."

- As the old song sings, "I sing because I'm happy, I sing because I'm glad, for His eye is on the sparrow and I know he watches me." Amen

Pray

Eternal God, our Heavenly Father! As long as we live on this earth, we will sing your praise. As long as there is breath in our lungs, we will tell of your wonderful works. Until the day we die, we will glory in your holy name. Even though the storms come and people disappoint us, we will continue to give thanks because your goodness and steadfast love endures forever.

Keep us healthy and safe. Amen!

Listen and/or Sing

"His Eye Is on the Sparrow"
https://www.youtube.com/watch?v=MkTkfpOjoi8

Part 8

Faith talk while waiting for a hurricane!

"My times are in your hand." Psalm 31:15 (NRSV)

### "In God's Hands"

Several years ago, now, a French minister and a professor preached "My times are in your hand" during a New Years' service at a Reformed Church in North Africa. It was a warm and meaty sermon, stirring and alive. It was also his last. Five days later, when he returned to Paris, he died quiet unexpectedly from a heart attack.

Life is fragile. No one knows what the next day holds. We all hope and pray that there will be another day for us, but we simply cannot be sure about tomorrow. Therefore, it is comforting to read in Psalm 31:15 that "my time" (and "your time") are in God's hand--not in the hand of some blind and cruel fate but in the hand of our loving God who cares about me/you and what happens to us.

Yes, Loving God, "My times are in your hand." Thank you for reminding me/us of this great and wonderful truth.

Pray

Good morning, Father God! What a week! The memories and images are powerful and distressing. Send your Son into our midst even now so that the glorious hope of Christ will become as clear as the shining sun on the brightest day. Let us see what we have not yet seen, know what we have not yet known, experience that peace of Christ which passes all understanding.

O Lord, send your protection to all who are in Storm Irma's path of destruction.

Sing and/or Listen

"Because He Lives"

https://www.youtube.com/watch?v=spa7WkwjwGw

After the Storm

Faith Talk

Part 9

Faith talk while waiting for a hurricane!

"O LORD, our Sovereign, how majestic is your name in all the earth! You have set your glory above the heavens." Psalm 8:1

"The Glory of God"

This is the time to focus on the glory of God. Other things may change around us but the glory of God never changes. It has not been diminished by Hurricane Irma nor the one coming.

Some people do not see the glory of God; others deny the fact of it; but God's glory in nature is clear to many of us. I know I see it and celebrate it and I suspect you do so as well.

Several years ago, Joan and I stood on the rim of the Grand Canyon. We were amazed to see that massive crater extended before us as far as we could see. The colors and shapes "blew us out of the water." We had never seen anything like it. Needless to say, we experienced the glory of God.

The universe is exploding with the glory of God. On both the macro and micro levels, in both human and non-human creatures, the cosmos overflows with life, with complexity, with music, and with movement.

Like the Psalm writer, we stay focused on the glory of God. Hymns, anthems, prayers, scriptures, psalms, sermons, and worship services are instruments for that.

Planet earth did not end the night Irma attacked. The universe is still in place, a magnificent creation of God. Moreover, the universe continues to reflect the glory of its Creator, the Lord God Almighty.

Pray

Eternal God, our Heavenly Father! As long as there is breath in our lungs, we will tell of your wonderful works. Until the day we die, we will glory in your holy name. Even though the storms come and people disappoint us, we will continue to give thanks because your goodness and steadfast love endure forever.

Sing and/or Listen

"O Worship the King"

https://www.youtube.com/watch?v=SpPy5ZFAeKI

Part 10

Faith talk in the aftershock of a hurricane!

"As a deer longs for flowing streams, so my soul longs for you, O God. My soul thirsts for God, for the living God. When shall I come and behold the face of God?" Psalm 42: 1

"I really missed church last Sunday!"
In anticipation of Hurricane Irma, our church services were cancelled last Sunday, September 10. I really missed it. I missed seeing members of my church family. I missed the feeling that I get during the worship service. I missed singing the hymns, praying the prayers, and listening to the sermon. Moreover, I missed feeling close to God. I missed it all. All day Sunday, I felt like a part of me was missing. I want more than anything to go back and look forward to next Sunday.

Let me be clear. I do not worship God because I feel good; some Sundays I feel really tired. I do not show up at church because everything is going great; sometime things are not going well. I do not worship to persuade God to do something for me; God loves me/us unconditionally. I do not show up in church to persuade God to save me; because God has already saved me/us through Jesus Christ. I do not worship so that God will magically make hurricanes disappear; God is not a magician. I do not show up in church because I am pious; I know better.

I will show up in church this Sunday to "behold the face of God." This is a metaphor for worship. Like the Psalmist of old, I too hunger and thirst to experience the presence of God in the worship of the church family. Thank God for Sanlando United Methodist Church.


### Pray

Loving God! We are your children who share the common heritage of your steadfast love. Grant us the strength needed to bear our burdens, courage to face the uncertainty of the future, and confidence to place our trust in your will. Moreover, empower us with an energized faith and with strength, courage, and hope in Christ. Amen.

Sing and/or Listen
"Near to the Heart of God"
https://www.youtube.com/watch?v=2UnFNHWJ0tA

"There is a place of quiet rest,
near to the heart of God;
a place where sin cannot molest,
near to the heart of God.
Refrain:
O Jesus, blest Redeemer,
sent from the heart of God,
hold us who wait before thee
near to the heart of God."
-The United Methodist Hymnal Number 472
Cleland B. McAfee

Part 11

Faith talk in the aftershock of a hurricane!

Christ among us!

We have a friend in Jesus!

"For where two or three are gathered in my name, I am there among them." Matthew 18:20

"Our Friend"

Does anyone remember the song, "You've Got A Friend." It was written by Carole King. I heard it recently, once again. Suddenly, I realized why it was so popular in those days. It promises unqualified, unlimited, unconditional friendship. If you are lonely or in trouble, the song says, just call my name and I'll come to you. That's quite a commitment. There are a few people in life upon whom we can count to be that open to us whenever we have needs.

If fortunate, you have a handful of family members and friends who would be there for you in the midst of adversity. As we get older that list may dwindle, but the Bible tells us that all have at least one friend always. He is among us today. Christ Jesus, it is he. If you have a problem today too big to handle, he is there with you. You've got a friend in him.

"What a friend we have in Jesus! All our sins and griefs to bear!" Yes, of course. Christ the King among us during the storm. To Him be glory and honor, adoration and praise, now and forevermore. Amen.

### Pray

Dear Jesus! Even in my limited understanding of life, I stand in awe of your mercy. It's like the air I breathe to sustain me, like the sun that warms me, like the raindrops that renew me. Wherever I look, wherever I am, whatever I do, in the church family I experience your great mercy. Thank you, Jesus, for being my eternal friend. Amen.

Sing and/or Listen
"Leave It There"
https://www.youtube.com/watch?v=iXi3gpVRbCc

"Leave It There"

"If the world from you withhold
of its silver and its gold,
and you have to get along with meager fare,
just remember in his Word
how he feeds the little bird,
take your burdens to the Lord and leave it
there.
Leave it there, leave it there,
take your burden to the Lord and leave it there.
If you trust and never doubt,
he will surely bring your out;
take your burden to the Lord and leave it
there."

-Charles Albert Tindley.
The United Methodist Hymnal, No. 522.

In the Aftershock of the Storm

Faith Talk

Part 1

Faith talk in the aftershock of a hurricane!

"Bless the Lord, O my soul, and all that is within me, bless his holy name. Bless the Lord, O my soul, and do not forget all his benefits." Psalm 103: 1-2

### "Bless the Lord"

After Hurricane Irma had unleashed her fury on us, there was destruction everywhere. Duke Power announced in an email that power had been replaced to 809,000 customers. Joan and I were not among the fortunate ones. I'm grateful for all who were so blessed but we were not. Nevertheless, we did not complain. Rather we chose to bless the Lord and forget not his benefits.

It is true, of course, that one might have some other motives for showing up in church on the Sunday after a hurricane, but blessing the Lord was/is the main reason.

People go to church for many reasons. It is true that some go to church seeking blessings from God.

- Some people get in the prayer line for a blessing.

- Some people give offerings to get a blessing.

- Some people sing hymns to get a blessing.

- Some people study the Bible to get a blessing.

People come to church to get a blessing. But there's a challenge in Psalm 103. This Word of God calls us to bless God who has already blessed us! The purpose of worship (vs 3-8) is to "bless the Lord." That's the reason for hymns, psalms, doxologies, prayers, anthems, sermons, and benedictions.

I have noted through a half century of ministry that a host of people just won't give up, shut up, let up, until they have stayed up, stored up, prayed up, paid up, preached up, and blessed up the Lord.

I especially appreciated the little child, the last one to leave the children's moments with the pastor for children's church. She cried out, "Praise the Lord." Can't beat that. In fact, that is the last statement of the Book of Psalms.

## Pray

We praise you, O God, for making your Word the Word of life and sending Jesus to save us. Amen

## Sing and/or Listen

"10,000 Reasons"

https://www.youtube.com/watch?v=RtL_xeRoyVU

Practice the Spiritual Discipline of Journaling

A way to concentrate on being in Christ's presence during a hurricane.

1. Read the devotion/reflection for the day. Record your thoughts and/or write your personal reflections.

2. Be still and prayerfully listen for Christ's message to you. Record what you hear from the Lord.

3. Pray the prayer that is written and/or record and pray your own prayer.

4. Conclude with praise and worship. Use the suggested hymn from YouTube or choose another.

Part 2

Faith talk in the aftershock of a hurricane!

It is reassuring in a hurricane to know that we are precious to Jesus!

Read Mark 1:21-28

"Jesus is for Us"

In view of a hurricane's destructive power, here is the question, "Jesus of Nazareth, what have you to do with us?" Are you for us or against us? Do you want to destroy us or save us?

When the man in the gospel story asked this timely and timeless question, he was passionate. Suddenly, that pathetic, psychotic man jumped center stage. Getting right up in Jesus' face, he shouted, "What have you to do with us, Jesus of Nazareth? Have you come to destroy us?" He wanted to know about Christ's motives, especially in relationship to himself.

Some people today are not sure as to whether Jesus intends good or harm. Others could care less. The poor man in the gospel, however, cried out passionately to Jesus, "have you come to destroy us?" Absolutely not!

Here is the gospel reality. Every person is precious to Jesus! No one so bad, no one so sick, no one so worthless that he/she is locked out, blocked out, or shut out from Christ's grace. The truth is that Jesus' motive is to save, not destroy.

The poor man in the gospel cried out to Jesus, "have you come to destroy us?" Absolutely not. It is clear in the gospel that Christ is not an all-powerful cosmic umpire who delights in striking people out and throwing them out of the game. To the contrary, "God sent not his Son to condemn the world, but that the world might be saved through him." (John 3:17) Therefore, we don't have to beg or bribe Jesus to have mercy on us. Jesus is not an obstinate, cosmic umpire. Not at all!

Jesus is our loving Savior who has a heart for each and every one of us. This theme runs throughout New Testament. Therefore, any suggestion that a hurricane Irma is punishment from Jesus and God is absolute nonsense. Amen.

## Pray

Dear Jesus, I rejoice that each person is of such great value to you, apart from anything he/she does.

It is true Lord - isn't it? - that you value each one as a person of inestimable worth.

It is true - isn't it Lord? - that there's nothing to prove, that no one has to earn your love.

It is true - isn't it Lord? - that human worth is given as a birthright because we are made in the image of God, your Heavenly?

## Prayer

Thank you, Dear Jesus, for loving me, as well as all others, as demonstrated by your death on the cross for the salvation of the world. Amen

## Sing and/or Listen

"I Stand Amazed"

https://www.youtube.com/watch?v=S7QuZ4wo1X4

Part 3

Faith talk in the aftershock of a hurricane!

Friends matter during the aftershock of a hurricane.

Job 2:11-13

## "The Ministry of Presence"

We know people who have suffered greatly as a hurricane unleashes its fury against us. Some will die; others will be injured; others will lose their homes; others will lose their source of income; others will lose electricity and be subjected to sweltering heat without air-conditioning; others will experience severe property damage; and almost everyone in the hurricane's path will experience major disruptions. Some will even live a modern-day version of the story of the biblical Job.

Read Job's story again (Job 1 & 2). He lost everything, not only his wealth and health but also his children. Word of his trouble spread quickly. Three friends showed up to comfort him. They overflowed with empathy, sympathy, and compassion. For seven days and nights the three friends sat with Job, prayed and supported him, but they did not say a word, not one word, not even a "mumbling word."

That's a compelling picture of the "Ministry of Presence." The three friends were attentive and courteous, warm and embracing, loving and supportive.

The "Ministry of Presence" is a comforting ministry. Nevertheless, it is hard to be present and caring when someone is overwhelmed with grief as well as doom and gloom, but this ministry is a gift from the Lord.

I am thankful that the Lord has provided friends, like the friends of Job, who are "present" to friends and neighbors who are still over-whelmed, even after a Hurricane is long gone.

These friends have called to assure you are OK. Moreover, they have come and sat with you, prayed with you, and supported you. And when you were too grief stricken and overwhelmed to speak, they did not panic and flee; rather, they sat with you, held your hand, and let you cry.

A favorite gospel story picture of Jesus prac-ticing the "Ministry of Presence" is the story of Lazarus (John 11:1-36). In fact, when Jesus went to Mary's and Martha's home, he wept when Mary told him that her brother Lazarus had died. The profound grief of the whole community got to him. And the gospel says that "He was deeply moved in spirit and troubled." Jesus wept.

The "Ministry of Presence" is a comforting ministry. You are invited to join Christ and prac-tice it in the aftermath of the coming storm.

Sign or/and Listen

"Lord, I want to be like Jesus in my heart."

https://www.youtube.com/watch?v=GvGK6AYsfrU


"Lord, I want to be like Jesus in my heart, in my heart,
Lord, I want to be like Jesus in my heart, in my heart.
In my heart, in my heart,
Lord, I want to be like Jesus in my heart, in my heart."

-The United Methodist Hymnal


Pray

Lord, thank you for persons who practice the Ministry of presence. Help me, help us to practice it, just like Jesus. Amen.

Part 4

Faith talk in the aftershock of a hurricane!

"Neither life nor death nor anything else in all creation can separate us from the love of God in Christ Jesus our Lord." Read Romans 8:31,38-39

### "The Question?"

Here is the question: "If God is for us, who is against us?"

Well, the coming hurricane for one. No! No! Not a woman but a hurricane named Irma in 2017. She may even have been the worst storm in our country's history. She caused staggering damage to us, billions of dollars state wide. Moreover, she caused injury and death to young and old, and disrupted our lives unmercifully. Our streets were littered with tree limbs and obstructed by dead oak trees. My electric power was dead for a week and the county warned of a possible sewage back up. Irma did not do us a favor. In fact, her assault was clearly against us. We spent months recovering.

What is the answer to the question?

One thing Irma did not and could not do was/is to separate us from the Love of God. The inescapable truth is that "Neither life nor death nor anything else in all creation can separate us from the love of God in Christ Jesus our Lord."

On the "Lord's Day," as we lived with the aftershock of Irma, we gathered with our church family to celebrate God's unconditional love. Nothing, absolutely nothing, can separate us from it.

### Pray

Lord, there are just some things that cannot be done. A hurricane cannot separate us from your love. Moreover, no one can empty the immeasurable ocean of God's love. No church, no creed, and no mind is big enough to measure or exhaust the love of God as revealed to us in Christ Jesus. We stand amazed in the face of your love. Amen.

Sing and/or Listen

"O Love That Wilt Not Let Me Go"

https://www.youtube.com/watch?v=hNovIpiqxAs

"O Love that Wilt Not Let Me Go"
*O Love that wilt not let me go,*
*I·rest my weary soul in thee;*
*I give thee back the life I owe,*
*That in thine ocean depths its flow*
*May richer, fuller be.*

George Matheson
*The United Methodist Hymnal,* No. 480

Part 5

Faith talk in the aftershock of a hurricane!

Is Jesus weeping with us and for us as we are in
the hurricane's destructive path?

John 11: 33-37

"Jesus Wept"

The first Bible verse I learned as a child is "Jesus
wept." I'm not surprised that it may also be the first
verse you learned as well.

The gospel story of Lazarus opens to us the heart
of Jesus Christ. Lazarus was young man who died unexpectedly and prematurely. His sisters expected
him to live a long life, marry, and have children and
grandchildren. Moreover, they expected him to die a
happy old man, but Lazarus died young from natural
causes. Understandably, Lazarus' sisters, Martha and
Mary, were broken hearted, grief stricken, and numb
with sorrow, just as we are in view of reports that

some died during Hurricane Irma, such as the elderly residents of a nursing home in Hollywood, FL.

The whole community was in grief, too, just as our community is. How could it be otherwise with victims, dead much too soon? Doesn't seem right. Doesn't seem fair. Doesn't seem just.

Like Martha and Mary, Jesus was broken hearted, grief stricken, and numb with sorrow. In fact, Jesus wept when Mary told him that her brother Lazarus had died. The profound grief of the whole community got to him. And the gospel says that "He was deeply moved in spirit and troubled."

The gospel image of Jesus weeping is powerful. Isn't this a picture of the heart of our Lord? Therefore, we are confident that every heartbreaking victim of Irma's wrath is covered by his tears. We are confident that Jesus weeps for those poor victims and for us just as he wept for Lazarus.

Picture this: we will be bathed in the tears of Jesus in the aftershock of the coming hurricane. Jesus wept when they told him about the death of Lazarus. In your mind's eye, picture Jesus also weeping for all the victims who will suffer from the storm. Amen.

### Pray

Lord I/we love this image, "Jesus Wept." That's what we have to hold onto as the storm barrels down on us. Your love, the love of God, is not only for Lazarus but also for all in harm's way. As the community said, seeing your tears for Lazarus, "See how he loves him!" I affirm that you also love all who are in danger. Thank you, Jesus, for the depth of your love.

### Sing and/or Listen
"Give Me Jesus"
https://www.youtube.com/watch?v=P37bM87b9pg

Practice the Spiritual Discipline of Journaling

A way to concentrate on being in Christ's presence during a hurricane.

1. Read the devotion/reflection for the day. Record your thoughts and/or write your personal reflections.

2. Be still and prayerfully listen for Christ's message to you. Record what you hear from the Lord.

3. Pray the prayer that is written and/or record and pray your own prayer.

4. Conclude with praise and worship. Use the suggested hymn from YouTube or choose another.

Part 6

Faith talk in the aftershock of a hurricane!

## Who is blessed? Matthew 5: 1-12

### "Blessed!"

After seven nights of darkness and without air conditioning, the power was finally restored to our house. I must say that Joan and I felt blessed. Nevertheless, we wondered. Why us?

A friend asked, why you and not us? Indeed! Is "power back on" a blessing from God or Duke Energy? We give God "the glory" to be sure, in this as in all things. And we also give our electric company glory but not "the glory" we reserve for God

Who is blessed? Are you? Am I? How about the people who did not lose power during hurricane Irma, or whose property was not damaged, or who did not suffer death or injury?

Who is blessed? Jesus teaches us in the "Beatitudes." One group is the poor in spirit.

"Blessed are the poor in spirit," he states in the gospel, "for theirs is the kingdom of heaven."

That's how "the poor in spirit" are blessed. The kingdom of heaven is given to them and lives within them now.

- Through the storm and through the rain, the kingdom of heaven is within them.

- Through the good times and the bad, the kingdom of heaven is within them.

- When death arrives, and takes their loved ones home, the kingdom of heaven is within them.

- When the wind blows down their trees and rips the roof from their house, the kingdom of heaven is within them.

- When they lose power in their home and the air conditioner stops working, the kingdom of heaven is within them.

- When the thunder clears her throat in the heavens, and the lightening rips across the midnight sky, the kingdom of heaven is within them.

Why? What did they do to deserve the kingdom? Nothing, absolutely nothing! Nor can you and I earn it. Rather, the kingdom of heaven is Christ's gracious gift to the poor in spirit.

### Pray

I give thanks to you, Lord, for your kingdom which is within me. You chose me through Holy Baptism. I seek from you, Lord God, the strength needed to keep on keeping on. Keep me from discouragement. Keep me focused on living today with joy and hope, with purpose and meaning, remembering to give thanks for all your blessings. Amen.

### Sing and/or Listen

"I Love Thy Kingdom, Lord"

https://www.youtube.com/watch?v=oAgygGKeKgI

Part 7

Faith talk in the aftershock of a hurricane!

### The Beatitudes Matt. 5:1-12

"Blessed are those who mourn for they will be comforted." (v.4

### "Comforted"

Is it true? As "the poor in spirit" pass through the aftershock of a hurricane, are they being comforted. Moreover, how and when and where is this happening?

What does comforted mean? Does it mean one's loss will be reversed? Does it mean Jesus will make your loss up to you?

Sometimes things just don't work out good for devout people. The fact is that devout people have suffered great misfortune during hurricane Irma. That is the current reality!

The Lord does not delay comfort to life after death. Of course, one will be comforted after one's death but that is not the point. Rather, Jesus promises, "they will be comforted," as a present reality.

Think of it like this. Jesus has surrounded us with a church family. I have observed and experienced "comfort" from the family of Christ during this time of loss, just as Christ intended. My guess is that you have as well.

This comfort has and is taking shape in every Florida church family in various ways during the aftershock of any hurricane. The family supports those experiencing loss with food, diapers for babies, shelter, yard clean-up, transportation, prayers, phone calls, pastoral visits, and Holy Communion. The support is loving, comforting, and helpful.

During the aftershock of Hurricane Irma, victims were comforted by the local church family Jesus has established. I must say that in times like this, I'm so glad to be a part of the family of Christ.

Pray

I know I have made mistakes in my life. I have rebelled against your holy commandments and violated your rules for a godly life. I have not kept the Ten Commandments; nor have I loved my neighbor as myself. I regret much that I have done and said even during this last week.

Despite my failures in the past, you have forgiven my sins and have given me a church family where I am truly comforted by the encouragement and prayers of those who love me for your sake. Amen.

Sing and/or Listen

"The Family of God"

https://www.youtube.com/watch?v=xlT6KoT73O0

Practice the Spiritual Discipline of Journaling

A way to concentrate on being in Christ's presence during a hurricane.

1. Read the devotion/reflection for the day. Record your thoughts and/or write your personal reflections.

2. Be still and prayerfully listen for Christ's message to you. Record what you hear from the Lord.

3. Pray the prayer that is written and/or record and pray your own prayer.

4. Conclude with praise and worship. Use the suggested hymn from YouTube or choose another.

Part 8

Faith talk in the aftershock of a hurricane!

The Beatitudes, Matt. 5:1 12 (v.5)
"Blessed are the meek."

### "The Meek"

Early in the aftermath of Irma, I asked a friend, "How are you today?" She replied, "I'm blessed!" By that, she meant that electricity had been restored to her house. I rejoiced with her, even though mine and thousands of other Floridians' had not yet been restored.

That got me to wondering. Who is blessed? So, I asked Jesus. "The meek" he replied. "Blessed are the meek."

Hmm! Who is meek? Not the weak-kneed and fearful person. Not the doormat person! But the person who is submissive to the will of Christ.

Consider these examples. Think of Peter, James, John, Mark, and all the disciples. They were strong and courageous men to be sure, and they were submissive to the will of Christ.

The "meek" Apostles chose to be obedient to Christ and chose to suffer abuse and even death as Christ did for the sake of the gospel.

Like the "meek" Apostles, present day Christians may choose to be "meek" and live through the aftershock of Hurricane Irma, loving God and neighbors in obedience to the gospel of Christ.

Is this smart? Does it really pay to be "meek" like Jesus and live for him in a time like this? "Blessed are the meek," said Jesus, "for they shall inherit the earth."

Sing and/or Listen

"Living for Jesus"
https://www.youtube.com/watch?v=rChnJ15-mj0

Prayer

Dear Jesus, I want to be meek, just like Peter and Mark and Matthew and all of the Holy Apostles. I want to be meek, just as you were during your earthly pilgrimage. Give me the courage and reinforce within me the will to be meek. Amen.

Part 9

Faith talk in the aftershock of a hurricane!

The Beatitudes Matt. 5:1 12 (v.6) "Blessed are those who hunger and thirst for righteousness, for they will be filled."

## "Hunger for Righteousness"

Is righteousness what I want? Is this what you want? Do you, do I, do we hunger and thirst for righteousness?

This is not to ask whether I or you hunger and thirst to be a good person. Rather, it is to ask whether we yearn for God's righteousness. Think of it like this. God's righteousness is immovable. It stays in place. It does not move to the left or the right. It does not favor any nation or political party. God's righteousness is the right option as we struggle with political, economic, and moral confusion.

God's righteousness is not just good advice. Rather, it is the standard to which we must adjust, and apart from which human existence will not turn out right.

Is that what we really want? "Blessed are those who hunger and thirst after (God's) righteousness," said Jesus. So what? "They will be filled." Well, yes of course! You will be filled.

• Filled with the moral and spiritual compass to guide you through.

• Filled with the moral and spiritual rudder to steer your course.

• Filled with the values to navigate the midnight of confusion and despair.

Here is what I want. "I want a principle within of watchful, godly fear."

Sing and/or Listen
"I want a principle within"
https://www.youtube.com/watch?v=Yk2b9XMZYRA

Pray

Lord, I want a principle within of watchful, godly fear. I want to love you with my whole heart and to love my neighbors as myself. Lord, have mercy on me and grant my request to hunger and thirst after your righteousness. Amen

Part 10

Faith talk in the aftershock of a hurricane!

"Merciful"

The Beatitudes, Matt. 5:1-12
"Blessed are the merciful, for they shall obtain mercy." (v.7)

Who is blessed? Jesus said, 'Blessed are the merciful." Hmmm? Who are these merciful?

Note that the preposition "if" is not in this beatitude. Jesus does not say, "If you live an exemplary life and are a patriotic American, you will receive mercy." Rather, he says, "Blessed are the merciful, for they will receive mercy."

Good news!

- You don't have to have a college degree to be merciful.
- You don't have to be an ordained minister or priest to be merciful.

- You don't have to make your subjects and your verbs agree to be merciful.
- You don't have to be a Republican or a Democrat to be merciful.
- You don't have to be young or old to be merciful.
- You only need a heart full of grace and goodwill.
- A heart that cares for "the least" is a heart that pleases Jesus.

When it comes to being merciful,
- Nationality doesn't matter,
- Race doesn't matter.
- Blood lines don't matter.
- Even being Methodist doesn't count for much here either.

What really matters, according to Jesus parable of the last judgement, is the kindness and compassion which are extended to the "least among us."

Good news! The merciful will receive mercy. That's not my verdict. Not at all. That is the Word of the Lord. Amen.

## Pray

Dear Jesus, I understand that you desire mercy. Yes, mercy as in respect for each person's personal dignity. Help me to welcome all into your family, encouraging them as they live through their personal heartache, standing by them when they are out of money, out of physicians, out of hope, and out of people to minister to them. Yes, I would be merciful to the bedraggled, beat-up and burnt out people of the world! Help me to be merciful as you were merciful during your earthly journey. Amen

## Sing and/or Listen

" Lord Whose Love in Humble Service"

https://www.youtube.com/watch?v=n8E1YbqY720

## Part 11

Faith talk in the aftershock of a hurricane!


### The Beatitudes
### Matt. 5:1-12

"Blessed are the merciful, for they shall obtain mercy." (v.7)

'Blessed are the merciful."

Jesus said, 'Blessed are the merciful." Hmm? Who are these merciful?

Each day is fraught with opportunities to be merciful. How do you respond? How do I respond? Do we show mercy or withhold it?

The Lord assures God's mercy to the merciful.

Moreover, in his great prayer, Jesus teaches us to pray, "forgive us our trespasses as we forgive those who trespass against us."

## Pray

Loving God! Even in our limited understanding of life, we stand in awe of your mercy. It's the air we breathe, the sun that warms us, the raindrops that renew us. Wherever we look, wherever we are, whatever we do, we experience your great mercy.

Lord, help me to be merciful as you are merciful. Make me forgiving and loving in all things. Teach me how to forgive, how to be merciful, how to be like Jesus. Amen.

## Sing and/or Listen

Great is thy Faithfulness
https://www.youtube.com/watch?v=N-HszBrTGfA

Part 12

Faith talk in the aftershock of a hurricane!

Who is blessed?

The Beatitudes
"Blessed are the pure in heart, for they shall see God." Matt. 5:1-12 (v.7)

"Who is pure in heart?"
As we recover from Irma, who is blessed? Jesus says the pure in heart are.

Hmm? Who are these "pure in heart?" Well, you are not "pure in heart" because you are such a good person. Rather, you are "pure in heart" because you have a one-track-mind, so to speak. i.e., You are single-minded, free of mixed motives, totally focused on Jesus and God's will.

Does this mean you are blessed? Yes, of course! Think about it like this. You pure in heart are blessed, because you shall see God -

- You shall see God in the faces of the poor and hungry,

- You shall see God in the sacrament of Holy Communion.
- You shall see God in the preaching of the gospel,
- You shall see God in the kingdom of Heaven.

"Blessed are the pure in heart for they will see God." Yes! Of course! You already do, see God in a way that others do not. Moreover, when life ends, you will see God in God's heaven!

Must we say it again? Death is not the end for "the pure in heart." They will see God in the great beyond.

Pray

Lord, I confess that this old expressway of my religious life has become obsolete through neglect, with deep valleys and lumpy hills, dusty corners and rough surfaces. Have mercy on me and descend upon my heart just now. Mold me and make me pure in heart.

Sing and/or listen
"Spirit of the Living God"

https://www.youtube.com/watch?v=z1UGBRlR8tI

## Part 13

Faith talk in the aftershock of a hurricane!

Are you blessed? Am I?

### The Beatitudes
### Matt. 5:1-12

"Blessed are the peacemakers, for they shall be called children of God." (v.9)

### "The Peacemakers"

Who is blessed? Jesus does not say "blessed are the deal makers, for they will be rich." Rather, he said, "Blessed are the peacemakers, for they shall be called children of God."

Who are the peacemakers? Well, these are disciples who actively work to reconcile people and enlarge the area of human goodwill. These are Christians who build bridges of understanding and compassion between individuals and individuals, tribes and tribes, nations and nations, Christian and non-Christian religions, as well as denominations.

114

Does peacemaking really matter to me and for me? Yes! Of course. Ask Jesus! Says he, "Blessed are the peacemakers, for they shall be called children of God."

When? Now! His promise is now coming true. The Lord means now, children of God, now!

Rejoice! Give thanks! And praise the Lord! "Let there be peace on earth and let it begin with me."

### Pray

Loving God, bring healing to those who are sick. Bring peace to those who are afraid. Bring hope to those who face discouragement. Bring joy to those who face sorrow.

Knowing the pain some endure, I bring their cries and concerns to you. I pray especially for those who want to do the right thing, but who are prevented by community attitudes and even the laws of our state. Lord have mercy. Amen.

### Sing and/or listen
"Let There Be Peace on Earth"
https://www.youtube.com/watch?v=1BkoaPTeZM0

Part 14

Faith talk in the aftershock of a hurricane!

How long must one serve to qualify for eternal life?

Read Matthew 20: 1-16.

### "Grace"

The parable of the "Laborers in the Vineyard" pulls into focus two worlds in the church family which come upon us with great power. Or, perhaps I should say, two worlds which impact our lives significantly.

On the one hand is this world of economics. On that side are laborers in the vineyard. On that side are grapes and workers. On that side, there are contracts and wages. On that side, there are children to be fed and educated. On that side, the rule is "a full day's pay for a full day's work."

On the other side of our experience is this other world of grace. On that side, things are quite different. On that side, the rule of "a full day's pay for a full day's work" does not apply. At the end of the day, everyone receives the same pay. It doesn't matter whether one has worked for eight hours or one. This is the world of "Amazing Grace."

God's kingdom rules are radically different from the secular world's? The key is the loving heart of our Heavenly Father. The first last and the last first.

The point of the parable is the graciousness and generosity of God. God is gracious and generous to a fault. Like it or not, that's the way it is in God's kingdom within the church family, just as it is in heaven.

At the end of the day, the compensation for a person who dies on the day he commits to Christ is as great as for a Christian who has labored for fifty years in the Kingdom of God.

## Pray

Dear Jesus, I am grateful for your amazing grace. I have received countless blessing, big and small. I am fortunate to be supported and sustained by your loving presence. Even when I was faraway, like the Prodigal Son in the gospel, squandering my life in a far country, you waited for me, called to me, embraced me, and welcomed me home to the church. Moreover, I now receive and will receive more than I could possibly earn and deserve. Thank you for the gift of salvation. Amen.

Listen and/or Sing, "Freely, Freely"

https://www.youtube.com/watch?v=9-QcrKkXpcg

"He said 'Freely, freely you have received;
freely, freely give.
Go in my name, and because you believe others
will know that I live."
United Methodist Hymnal

Practice the Spiritual Discipline of Journaling

A way to concentrate on being in Christ's presence during a hurricane.

1. Read the devotion/reflection for the day. Record your thoughts and/or write your personal reflections.

2. Be still and prayerfully listen for Christ's message to you. Record what you hear from the Lord.

3. Pray the prayer that is written and/or record and pray your own prayer.

4. Conclude with praise and worship. Use the suggested hymn from YouTube or choose another.

Part 15

Faith talk in the aftershock of a hurricane!

God is gracious and generous to a fault!

Matthew 20: 1-16.

"God of Grace"

God's kingdom rules are radically different from the secular world's? The key is the loving heart of our Heavenly Father - the first last and the last first.

The point of the parable is the graciousness and generosity of God. Not surprising! God is gracious and generous to a fault. Like it or not, that's the way it is in God's kingdom within the church family, just as it is in heaven.

At the end of the day, the compensation for a person who dies on the day he commits to Christ is as great as for a Christian who has labored for fifty years in the Kingdom of God.

Tammy is a missionary in India who runs a home with 41 children. This is not an orphanage, but a ministry where children are loved by Christ.

Tammyma shared the story of Gopi, a young boy of 11 who had a very rough past. She had a conference with his teacher one day only to find out that Gopi had been hiding notes sent home from the teacher for more than a month. He was failing everything and getting into trouble at school. Tammyma was pretty upset with Gopi for hiding all of this from her.

Shortly thereafter, Gopi ran away. Since he lives in a city with millions of impoverished people, Tammyma and her staff were quite fearful for his safety. They immediately formed search teams to go out and look for Gopi. The staff found him and brought him to Tammyma. She sobbed as he told her, "I didn't think you would ever come looking for me." She says, "It is the worst thing any kid has ever said to me. He simply did not know my heart for him." She had done so much for him, given so much, and yet, he didn't really know the depth of her love for him. [2]

Sadly, like little Gopi, we just don't know the depth of God's love for us. If only we could see and know God's heart for us. Whether we know it or not, God loves us unconditionally. God does not let go of us. That's the reason we still sing, "O love that Wilt not let me go."

## Pray

Our loving Heavenly Father, we have heard the good news of your unconditional love. We sing about it, preachers preach it, the church universal bears witness to it.

Where our faith in your love is weak, make it strong. Moreover, where our vision is dim, renew it, and where our hope is fragile, reinforce mind and spirit with your unconditional love.

---

2 Sat, Jan 29, 2005 David Yarborough, pastor of St. Simons Community Church. The Brunswick News

Help us to see into the depths of your loving heart as you have revealed it to us through the life and ministry of your Son Jesus Christ. Amen

Sing and/or Listen

"O Love That Wilt Not Let Me Go""

https://www.youtube.com/watch?v=hNovIpiqx
As

"O Love that wilt not let me go,
I rest my weary soul in thee;
I give thee back the life I owe,
That in thine ocean depths its flow
May richer, fuller be."
The United Methodist Hymnal, No. 480

## Epilogue

### "One Day at a Time, Sweet Jesus"

Irma came and went in 2017, leaving a path of destruction and suffering in her departure. No one bemoaned her passing. In fact, we all rejoiced that she moved on and finally died. Good riddance!

Did Jesus help us deal with life during the time Irma was with us? Of course! He was with us each moment of each day.

Before the storm, Jesus gave us the "Prayer" to pray before, during, and after the hurricane. This prayer was an alternative to prayers that try to manipulate God with flowery words, magical formulas, or endless chants. It did steer us away from prayers that are selfish, and it did help us receive what we really need, namely, Christ with us.

Not only during a hurricane but also through other storms, we worry needlessly - worry about big things and little, worry about the past, and worry about the future. We worry about our finances, worry about our family, worry about food and water.

Through it all, Jesus Christ was with us and present in his prayer used by people like us. This prayer from the lips of Jesus lifted minds and hearts up to our Heavenly Father "from whom all blessings flow."

Yes! "One Day at a Time, Sweet Jesus" Amen

Listen and/or Sing
https://www.youtube.com/watch?v=JhUvFqOY00I

"One day at a time, sweet Jesus
That's all I'm asking from You
Just give me the strength to do everyday
What I have to do

Yesterday's gone, sweet Jesus
And tomorrow may never be mine
Lord, help me today, show me the way
One day at a time."
- Lynda Randle

Practice the Spiritual Discipline of Journaling

A way to concentrate on being in Christ's presence during a hurricane.

1. Read the devotion/reflection for the day. Record your thoughts and/or write your personal reflections.

2. Be still and prayerfully listen for Christ's message to you. Record what you hear from the Lord.

3. Pray the prayer that is written and/or record and pray your own prayer.

4. Conclude with praise and worship. Use the suggested hymn from YouTube or choose another.

John 3:16-17

"For God so loved the world that he gave his only Son, so that everyone who believes in him may not perish but may have eternal life. Indeed, God did not send the Son into the world to condemn the world, but in order that the world might be saved through him." Amen.

Made in the USA
Columbia, SC
09 July 2018